SUMMARY: Factfulness

BY HANS ROSLING.

IN A NUTSHELL PUBLICATIONS

Table of Contents

Chapter One: The Gap Instinct

Rosling begins by talking about the gap instinct, which is the tendency by all humans to divide all things into two extremes, two distinct categories, with a space or gap in between. People always view things in a state of two conflicting groups – the rich and the poor, the haves and the have nots, us versus them, developed and developing countries, high income versus low income and so on. Placing everything into one of two categories is simple and makes it easy for us to develop a view of the world. According to Rosling, however, this view of the world is wrong and leads to a misleading perception of the world.

Rosling uses a number of examples to burst the myth that everything in the world is divided into two distinct groups. For instance, people talk about the developed world and the developing world. People in the 'developed world' supposedly have better access to healthcare, better education, longer life expectancy, and better access to electricity; while those from the 'developing countries' do not have access to all these. However, representing the actual data on access to healthcare, education, and electricity on a graph shows that most people have access to all these. Instead of most countries fitting in two distinct categories with a gap in between, most countries actually fall on the gap, with many of them moving towards the group of developed countries. Therefore, it makes no sense to describe the world in terms of developed and developing countries.

Instead of using the developed versus developing/high income versus low income worldview, Rosling introduces four categories that can provide us with a better view of the world, based on income levels. Level 1 consists of people who earn less than $2 per day. Level 2 is made up of people earning $2 - $8 a day. Level 3 is made up of people earning $8 - $32 a day, while people in Level 4 earn over $32 each day.

Generally, people within the same income level have a similar quality of life, regardless of where in the world they live. People in Level 1 have very low access to education and health, lower life expectancy, poor nutrition, live hand to mouth and rely on walking as their main mode of transport. People in Level 2 have improved nutrition, improved access to medication, might own a bicycle, might have access to electricity and can take their children to school. However, an emergency like a major illness will take them back to Level 1. People in Level 3 have even better access to health and education, better nutrition and are able to save for a rainy day, meaning that an emergency will not take them back to the previous level. People in Level 4 are rich consumers. They can afford a car, and foreign vacations. Education and healthcare for their family is not a problem. Using these four levels gives a better view of the world compared to dividing everything into two categories.

To avoid automatically using the two extremes mindset, Rosling provides three warning signs that you can use to recognize whenever your gap instinct is triggered. The first one is comparison of averages, where we use averages to compare between two situations. However, by comparing averages, we forget about the overlap that is in between the two situations, creating the illusion of a gap even where none exists. The second warning sign is the comparison of extremes, where we only compare extremes. Democracies versus oppressive dictatorship. The poorest versus the richest. Peaceful countries versus war-torn countries. This view is wrong simply because most countries and most people are in neither of these extremes. They exist in the space in between the two extremes. The third warning sign is what Rosling calls the view from above, where people from a higher income level look down on lower income levels without any familiarity to the kind of conditions within that level. For instance, people within Level 4 might think of people within Levels 1-3 as poor, even though those in Levels 2 and 3 are not really poor.

Throughout the rest of the book, Rosling uses the four income levels to explain all kinds of things and to help you get a much more accurate view of the world. He also reminds us that factfulness is recognizing that instead of things existing as two distinct groups with a gap in between, the reality is that there is no gap. The majority lies in the middle where the gap is supposed to be.

KEY TAKEAWAYS:

- People view things in a state of two conflicting groups.
- This view of the world is wrong and leads to a misleading perception of the world.
- Instead of using the developed versus developing/high income versus low income worldview, Rosling introduces four categories that can provide us with a better view of the world, based on income levels. Level 1 consists of people who earn less than $2 per day. Level 2 is made up of people earning $2 - $8 a day. Level 3 is made up of people earning $8 - $32 a day, while people in Level 4 earn over $32 each day.
- Generally, people within the same income level have a similar quality of life, regardless of where in the world they live.
- To avoid automatically using the two extremes mindset, Rosling provides three warning signs that you can use to recognize whenever your gap instinct is triggered:
- Comparison of averages.
- Comparison of extremes.
- The view from above.
- Factfulness is recognizing that instead of things existing as two distinct groups with a gap in between, the reality is that there is no gap. The majority lies in the middle where the gap is supposed to be.

Chapter Two: The Negativity Instinct

In this chapter, Rosling talks about the negativity instinct, which is the tendency by most humans to notice and pay attention to the bad rather than the good. The negativity instinct is the reason behind the great misconception by most people that the world is only getting worse. There might be some truth behind this mega conception. Today, terrorism is higher than it was 30 years ago. The environment is deteriorating at a faster rate than it was 30 years ago. However, despite such situations, the state of the world is generally getting better.

According to Rosling, the main reason why people think that the world is getting worse is because most improvements do not occur in leaps and bounds. Instead, the improvements occur gradually in small steps that are not worth reporting about. These small steps compound into great improvements that do not get reported. On the other hand, any minor setback receives great coverage, leading to the perception that the world is getting worse instead of better.

To illustrate the negativity instinct, Rosling uses several examples. In the 1800's, the majority of the world (85%) was at income Level 1, meaning extreme poverty was the norm rather than the exception. Today, only 9% of the world is at Level 1. Similarly, life expectancy has improved from 31 years in the 1800's to 72 years today. Several other improvements have taken place in the world compared to 200 years ago. Legal slavery was abolished, the number of HIV infections has decreased, child mortality has decreased, deaths in battle have decreased, plane crashes have decreased, child labor has decreased, hunger has decreased, more women have the right to vote, literacy and democracy have improved, access to education and electricity has increased, access to immunization has improved, access to water has improved, and so on. Despite all these improvements, the majority of people polled believe that the world is getting worse.

This tendency to notice the bad more than the good is caused by three things; misremembering the past, selective reporting and the feeling that it would be heartless to say that things are getting better when they are still bad in some places. When people start living a better life, they easily forget how bad things were previously. In addition, people tend to romanticize their youth, leading to the perception that things in the past were much better than they actually were.

Apart from misremembering the past, most of the news reported is negative – wars, famine, terrorism, corruption, natural disasters, accidents, and so on. A plane that makes a successful flight is hardly news material. However, a plane crash gets front page coverage across all newspapers. Today, it is also much easier to find out about bad events in far flung places than it was 30 or 50 years ago. Finally, the fact that problems still remain in the world make it appear heartless to claim that things are getting better. All these three factors combined lead to the erroneous perception that the world is getting worse.

Rosling proposes three ways to help control the negativity instinct. The first one is to persuade ourselves that bad and better are not mutually exclusive. That despite things being bad, it is still possible that they are better than they once were. Saying that things are better should not be confused with saying that things are fine. Second, we can control the negativity instinct by constantly expecting bad news. In a world where negative news is more likely to receive coverage than positive news, reminding yourself that there is more good happening that is not getting reported can help you control the negativity instinct. Finally, we can control the negativity instinct by not censoring or romanticizing history. The past was a lot worse than we think it was. However, accurately presenting history as it was can go a long way in helping us realize that we have come a long way, that there is a general trend of improvement. Factfulness is realizing that we are more likely to come across negative news, and remembering that there is more positive news out there that is not reaching us.

KEY TAKEAWAYS:

- The negativity instinct is the tendency by most humans to notice and pay attention to the bad rather than the good.
- The negativity instinct is the reason behind the great misconception by most people that the world is only getting worse.
- This tendency to notice the bad more than the good is caused by three things; misremembering the past, selective reporting and the feeling that it would be heartless to say that things are getting better when they are still bad in some places.
- Rosling proposes three ways to help control the negativity instinct. The first one is to persuade ourselves that bad and better are not mutually exclusive.
- Second, we can control the negativity instinct by constantly expecting bad news.
- Finally, we can control the negativity instinct by not censoring or romanticizing history.
- Factfulness is realizing that we are more likely to come across negative news, and remembering that there is more positive news out there that is not reaching us.

Chapter Three: The Straight Line Instinct

Rosling starts by talking about an Ebola outbreak in Liberia in 2014. Like most people, he assumed that the Ebola pandemic would be easily contained like most other disease outbreaks. He assumed that the number of new cases would keep increasing along a straight line, which made it possible for the disease to be easily stopped in its tracks. However, he came across a WHO report which said that the number of new cases was doubling, with every infected person infecting two more people on average before dying. The realization that the number of new cases was not increasing in a straight line is what spurred Rosling and the Gapminder Foundation into action.

To explain the significance of such exponential growth, Rosling talks about an old Indian legend about the game of chess. Asked to name a reward for beating the King at chess, Lord Krishna asks for rice, with a single grain of rice being placed on the first square of the chess board and then the number of grains being doubled for every consequent square.

Thinking the number will keep growing in a straight line, the King agrees to Lord Krishna's request. However, it takes the king a short while to realize that by the time he gets to the 64th square, the number of grains would be so high that the whole country of India cannot produce so much rice.

The straight line instinct is very evident in people's view of the world. For instance, many people, including those involved in planning for future sustainability of the world, assume that the world's population is just increasing. There is the misconception that if nothing is done, the world's population will get to unsustainable levels, thus creating the need for something drastic to be done in order to stem the rapid population growth. However, Rosling points out that, according to UN data, the rate of population growth keeps decreasing. As people earn better incomes and get better access to basic needs like healthcare and education, the number of children per family keeps decreasing. Therefore, there is no need for something drastic to be done. Instead, population growth can be controlled by reducing the levels of extreme poverty. Rosling compares this to the growth of his youngest grandchild. The boy grew by 7 inches in his first six months. Extrapolating his growth in a straight line would mean that the child would be 60 inches by his third birthday and 160 inches by his 10th birthday, which is impossible. Since we know the average height of a 3 or 10-year-old kid, we know that their height cannot keep growing in a straight line. However, when faced with unfamiliar situations, we tend to extrapolate and assume that the pattern will continue in a straight line.

To prevent or control the straight line instinct, Rosling urges the reader to keep in mind that curves naturally come in many different shapes, with straight lines being a lot less common. Things like the relationship between income levels and health, education, recreation or marriage age show a straight line. However, such relationships are not very uncommon. Instead, most relationships show other shapes, such as S curves, slides or humps. For instance, the relationship between primary level education and vaccination is an S curve. The relationship between income levels and number of babies per woman is a slide. The relationship between the income levels in a country and traffic deaths is a hump. Therefore, Rosling urges readers to avoid the instinct to assume that everything occurs in a straight line. We can only understand the progression of a phenomenon by understanding the shape of its curve. The assumption that we know how a phenomenon will progress beyond what we see can leads to erroneous conclusions, which will in turn lead to erroneous solutions. Factfulness is recognizing whenever we have the straight line instinct and reminding ourselves that straight lines rarely occur in reality.

KEY TAKEAWAYS:

- When faced with unfamiliar situations, we tend to extrapolate and assume that the pattern will continue in a straight line.
- To prevent or control the straight line instinct, Rosling urges the reader to keep in mind that curves naturally come in many different shapes, with straight lines being a lot less common.
- We can only understand the progression of a phenomenon by understanding the shape of its curve.
- Factfulness is recognizing whenever we have the straight line instinct and reminding ourselves that straight lines rarely occur in reality.

Chapter Four: The Fear Instinct

Rosling starts the chapter by discussing the happenings of October 7, 1975, when he was a junior doctor. An assistant nurse rushed into the examination room and told him that the survivors of a plane crash were being brought in to the hospital by helicopter. The senior hospital staff were out for lunch, meaning it would be up to him and the assistant nurse to handle the emergency, his first real emergency. In his panic at having to handle his first real emergency, Rosling confused the plane crash survivor for a Russian pilot. He was convinced that Russia was attacking Sweden. He confused color cartridge from the pilot's life jacket for blood, and was about to shred through a "G-Suit" worth over 10,000 Swedish Kroner had the head nurse not arrived in time. The fear and panic in his mind could not allow Rosling to see things for what they were.

Rosling goes on to explain that our minds have some kind of attention filter that filters out the things that get through to our mind. There is so much information out there that we would probably go insane trying to process it all. To keep us from getting paralyzed by too much information, our minds have developed a mental filter that only allows certain things to pass through. One of the things that pass through this filter are the dramatic and unusual occurrences. This explains why you will never see a newspaper headline about a meteorologist who correctly predicted the weather. Instead, newspapers are full of unusual and dramatic events such as earthquakes, terror attacks, floods, wars, disease, fires, and so on. The newspaper editors know that such events will pass through our attention filter. The problem is, the more of the unusual we see, the more we tend to believe that the unusual is usual.

The fear instinct developed and is hardwired into our brains as a result of millions of years of evolution. When our ancestors lived in the bush, the fear of physical harm, captivity and poisoning helped keep them alive. However, even though many of these dangers are no longer present, the perception of these dangers still remains. The fears are more relevant for people in Levels 1 and 2. For instance, people in Level 1 are more likely to be bitten by a snake. Since they do not have good access to healthcare facilities, it is a lot more sensible for a person in Level 1 to jump one time too many when they see a stick instead of getting bitten. However, for people in Level 4, the chances of getting bitten by a snake are much lower. Even if they got bitten, they have good access to health facilities, and therefore it is much less likely that they would lose their lives. For people in Level 4, these hardwired fears cause more harm than good, by distorting their view of the world.

The media knows that these fears are hardwired into our brains, which is why they keep tapping into these fears to grab our attention. In effect, this creates a paradox where the image of a dangerous world is being broadcast more effectively at a time when the world is safer than it has ever been before. The fears that kept our ancestors alive hundreds of years ago are the same ones keeping journalists employed today. For instance, today, the number of deaths from natural disasters has fallen significantly compared to 100 years ago. As countries move up from Level 1 towards Level Four, better infrastructure, better access to healthcare, better education and better disaster preparedness mean less people die from natural calamities. Organizations like the WHO and the UN step in to help victims of natural disasters, significantly reducing the number of deaths. Yet the people in Level 4, who are paying for the services of the WHO and the UN, are not aware of the success their efforts have achieved because the media keeps feeding them with news painting each disaster like the worst to ever happen in the world.

Rosling does not propose that we should smile in the face

of natural disasters and claim that the world is getting better. No. All efforts must be put to help the victims of natural disasters. However, once the immediate danger is over, it is important to cool down and look at things from a fact based approach. Doing so would make it easier to ensure effective use of resources against future suffering. For instance, the 2015 earthquake in Nepal that killed over 9000 people attracted a lot of attention. In the same year, Diarrhea caused by drinking contaminated water killed over 9000 children across the world. However, not much attention was paid to this cause of death, which occurs more frequently than an earthquake and requires much less resources to prevent compared to preventing and rescuing the victims of an earthquake.

Rosling talks about some of the improvements that have been made in the world. In 2016, the safest year in aviation history, only 10 flights, out of a total of 40 million flights, ended in fatal accidents. However, the fact that this was the safest year in aviation history was not worth reporting. Similarly, the number of deaths from battle has fallen greatly in the last 100 years, same as the threat of a nuclear war. However, none of these things get reported. Rosling talks about how, following the Tsunami in 2011, 1600 people died while escaping the province of Fukushima out of fear of radioactive contamination, while not a single person died of the actual thing they were running away from. He also talks about how the fear of chemicals like DDT leads to deaths that could have been prevented by DDT, which is a banned chemical despite the WHO and the CDC showing that DDT has more benefits than drawbacks. In both these cases, the fear of an invisible substance – DDT or radioactive contamination – leads to more harm than the substance itself. He also talks about terrorism, which causes far less deaths in the West than alcohol. Yet, terrorism receives greater coverage and resources than deaths caused by alcohol.

Rosling ends the chapter by noting that fear is a terrible guide for understanding the world. It makes us pay attention to things we are afraid of, even if there is not much risk from them, while ignoring things that are more likely to cause us harm. Fear can be a useful thing, but only if directed at the right things. Factfulness is learning to tell apart frightening things from dangerous things. Frightening things are a perceived risk, while dangerous things are an actual risk.

KEY TAKEAWAYS:

- To keep us from getting paralyzed by too much information, our minds have developed a mental filter that only allows certain things to pass through. One of the things that pass through this filter are the dramatic and unusual occurrences.
- The problem is, the more of the unusual we see, the more we tend to believe that the unusual is usual.
- The fear instinct developed and is hardwired into our brains as a result of millions of years of evolution.
- The fears are more relevant for people in Levels 1 and 2. For instance, people in Level 1 are more likely to be bitten by a snake and as they do not have access to good healthcare facilities they are at serous risk of injury/death.
- For people in Level 4, these hardwired fears cause more harm than good, by distorting their view of the world.
- The media knows that these fears are hardwired into our brains, which is why they keep tapping into these fears to grab our attention.
- Factfulness is learning to tell apart frightening things from dangerous things. Frightening things are a perceived risk, while dangerous things are an actual risk.

Chapter Five: The Size Instinct

Rosling starts this chapter by recounting about his time as a young doctor in Mozambique in the early 1980's, at a time when Mozambique was the poorest country. At the district hospital, they used to admit about 1000 children every year, on average, with one in every 20 children dying. One day, Rosling had an argument with a visiting friend about the kind of treatment being provided at the district hospital. According to Rosling, the only way to save more children was to provide better services outside the hospital. His friend, on the other hand, maintained that Rosling should have focused on providing the best care possible to the children that were brought to the hospital, instead of wasting time improving services outside the hospital.

This prompted Rosling to find the proportion of children who died within the hospital compared to those who died outside the hospital. He was surprised to find that while only slightly above 50 children died at the hospital died each year, over 3900 children died outside the hospital every year. Realizing that he was seeing only 1.3% of the work he was supposed to do, Rosling then went out and tried to introduce some form of basic care even for those children that could not get to hospital.

The size instinct is the tendency by humans to get things out of proportion. When looking at a single number exclusively, it is easy to misjudge its importance. For instance, when Rosling was saving 95% of the children who came to the hospital, it would have been easy to assume he was doing an exemplary job. However, comparing this to the number of children who were dying outside the hospital made him come to the realization that more needed to be done.

The size instinct is something that the media is very fond of. Journalists are always throwing out numbers at us and trying to impress on the populace how important these numbers are. The size instinct blows things out of proportion and leads to solutions that do not do much to help. For instance, in the situation at the district hospital in Mozambique, it would have been easy for politicians to assume that increasing the number of beds at the hospital would lead to less deaths. However, compared to the number of children dying outside the hospitals, it becomes clear that improving preventive care outside the hospital and improving access to education would lead to lesser deaths.

To avoid getting caught up in the size instinct, Rosling advises the reader to use the tools of comparison and division.

To explain why we should never judge a number on its own, he gives the example of the world's child mortality rate. In 2016, 4.2 million children died before the age of one. This seems like a very large number, and shows that a lot of effort needs to be put to lower the number of infant deaths. However, if you compare this with another number, you get a different picture. In 1950, 14.4 million babies died before their first birthday. This shows that the number of infant deaths has reduced greatly. However, looking at the 4.2 million figure by itself does not show this.

Rosling uses several other examples to illustrate how we tend to blow things out of proportion. A good example is the Vietnam War, which lasted 20 years and killed over 1.5 million Vietnamese. This seems like a very large number. However, Rosling was surprised to find that the Vietnamese monument for this war was no more than three feet high. He was astounded. However, the Vietnamese had built a huge monument in memory for their wars with China. The Wars with China had lasted 2000 years, and therefore, to them, a 20-year war was not worthy of much attention. Similarly, a Swedish hunter killed by a bear received more coverage than a Swedish woman hacked to death by her husband. Since death by bear is a rare occurrence, it was blown out of proportion by the media, while murder by a partner was barely covered because it is a frequent occurrence. Instead of getting concerned about murders by partners, which happen severely every year, the media was more concerned about something that was unlikely to happen again in the next several years, meaning it presented lesser risk.

In the same way, when Swine Flu broke out in 2009, it killed 31 people within 2 weeks. This created mass hysteria. The outbreak was covered massively in all news outlets. Within the same 2 weeks, over 63,000 people died from TB, yet there was little to no coverage of TB in the media.

Another tool Rosling uses to control the size instinct is the 80/20 rule. He says we should always look for the items that make up more than 80% of the total. For instance, if you look at the world's sources of energy – coal, gas, biofuels, solar, hydro, wind, oil, nuclear, geothermal – all might seem equally important. However, looking at the amount of energy they generate for humanity, it becomes clear that three of these – coal, gas, oil – generate more than 80% of the world's energy.

Every time you are faced with a single number that seems too important, Rosling urges you to divide it by a total in order to get a clearer picture of the situation. While amounts are easier to come up with, they are not very meaningful. If you want to get a better understanding of any situation, you should look for a rate (amount divided by a total). For instance, it might appear that China and India produce more CO_2 emissions than the USA and Germany respectively. However, dividing the amount of CO_2 emissions by the total population shows that USA and Germany emit more CO_2 per person than China and India.

To control the size instinct, Rosling urges the reader to get things in proportion by comparing or dividing with another relevant number. Factfulness is recognizing that a lonely number does not give a clear picture of any situation.

KEY TAKEAWAYS:

- The size instinct is the tendency by humans to get things out of proportion.
- The size instinct is something that the media is very fond of, journalists are always throwing out numbers at us and trying to impress on the populace how important these numbers are. The size instinct blows things out of proportion and leads to solutions that do not do much to help.
- To avoid getting caught up in the size instinct, Rosling advises the reader to use the tools of comparison and division.
- Another tool Rosling uses to control the size instinct is the 80/20 rule. He says we should always look for the items that make up more than 80% of the total.
- Every time you are faced with a single number that seems too important, Rosling urges you to divide it by a total in order to get a clearer picture of the situation.
- Factfulness is recognizing that a lonely number does not give a clear picture of any situation.

Chapter Six: The Generalization Instinct

In this chapter, Rosling starts by telling a story from his past. He decided to convince people from a remote village in Congo that it is against Swedish culture to eat larvae in a bid to avoid eating the larvae that the villagers had served to him as dessert. He then talks about the tendency of humans to categorize and generalize everything. This tendency to create categories is an important habit that helps us process information about the world. However, the habit can also distort our view of the world. Mistakenly placing people or things in the wrong category can lead to erroneous conclusions. Similarly, generalizing can lead us to attributing a certain characteristic to a whole group based on one unusual example. The generalization instinct is the reason behind stereotypes.

According to Rosling, generalizations are mind blockers. They might make you miss potential customers or producers for your product. For instance, after polling global financial experts, Rosling found that the majority assumed that a huge percentage of children below the age of one do not get vaccinated. Yet 80% of children below the age of one across the world get vaccinated. For the vaccines to get to these children, they need infrastructure for transportation, storage, electricity, health care, and education – the same infrastructure that is required for the establishment of factories. The fact that a majority of global financial experts believe that the majority of children are not vaccinated (when they are) shows they could be missing out on investment opportunities in some areas they consider as low income areas. Such a kind of generalization stems from the extreme deprivation that is presented in the news.

Rosling provides a number of solutions for controlling the generalization instinct. The first one is to travel. Traveling allows you to experience different places and cultures as they are and shows you that things are not as you might have assumed. The second way to get rid of the generalization is what he calls the Dollar Street, a project developed by his wife that shows photos of different aspects of daily life for different people based on their income levels. The third way of controlling the generalization instinct is to question your categories. You can question your categories through five major ways – looking for similarities across groups and similarities within groups, being skeptical of the term 'majority', being skeptical of exceptional examples, avoiding considering yourself as 'normal', and being aware whenever you find yourself generalizing one group from another.

Many people generalize African countries and talk about African problems, yet all the African countries are not at the same level. This leads to huge consequences, such as the Ebola pandemic in Liberia affecting tourism in Kenya, which is over 7000 kilometers away. The term majority is bad because it does not give any actual figures. Majority could be 51%, 76% or 99%. The term does not give an accurate representation of a situation. Exceptional examples also give a flawed picture. For instance, chemophobia is a result of generalization. It leads to the conclusion that most chemicals are harmful, when, in fact, most chemicals are beneficial. Assuming that you are normal can lead to generalizing others without understanding the reasons behind their behavior or actions. Remember, what is normal to you is not normal to them. Rosling closes the chapter by noting that factfulness is recognizing whenever categories are used and keeping in mind that categories can be misleading.

KEY TAKEAWAYS:

- Humans tend to categorize and generalize everything.
- The generalization instinct is the reason behind stereotypes.
- Generalizations are mind blockers.
- Rosling provides a number of solutions for controlling the generalization instinct:
- The first one is to travel. Traveling allows you to experience different places and cultures as they are and shows you that things are not as you might have assumed. The second way to get rid of the generalization is what he calls the Dollar Street, a project developed by his wife that shows photos of different aspects of daily life for different people based on their income levels. The third way of controlling the generalization instinct is to question your categories. You can question your categories through five major ways – looking for similarities across groups and similarities within groups, being skeptical of the term 'majority', being skeptical of exceptional examples, avoiding considering yourself as 'normal', and being aware whenever you find yourself generalizing one group from another.
- Exceptional examples also give a flawed picture.
- Factfulness is recognizing whenever categories are used and keeping in mind that categories can be misleading.

Chapter Seven: The Destiny Instinct

Rosling starts the chapter by recounting a time when he was presenting to a group of capital managers and their wealthiest clients at the Balmoral Hotel in Edinburgh. The aim of the presentation was to make it clear to the group that the emerging markets in Africa and Asia presented the greatest opportunities for profitable investments. However, despite all the data that he presented, at the end of the lecture a gray haired man came from the group and told him to his face that there was no chance the African countries would make it.

Rosling then introduces the destiny instinct, which is the tendency to assume that the destinies of people, cultures, countries or religions are determined by an innate characteristic of the group. This assumption leads to another greater assumption that there is nothing the people within the group can do to escape their destiny. The destiny instinct developed as a result of evolution. In the olden days, people lived in surroundings that didn't change much. Therefore, assuming that things would remain this way was a great survival skill, since they didn't have to constantly evaluate the surroundings.

In addition, creating the idea of a specific destiny for a specific group was a great way of uniting the group for a certain unchanging purpose, such as domination over other tribes. However, this instinct leads to a misconception of the world, since today's societies are constantly changing. However, the changes occur gradually, leading to the erroneous perception that no change is happening. To illustrate this point, Rosling points out that there is the erroneous perception that gender equality has not improved. However, statistics show that the average 30-year-old woman has spent just a year less in school compared to the average man of the same age.

This same assumption leads to the erroneous perception that European culture was destined to be superior to African and Asian cultures, hence the gentleman's argument that African countries would never catch up. However, the idea that Africa is destined to remain poor is based on feelings rather than fact. For instance, in the last 60 years, most African countries have reduced their infant mortality rate faster than Sweden did. 50 years ago, Asian countries were behind where most African countries are today, and it was assumed that they would never catch up and have the ability to feed 4 billion people. Yet today, many Asian countries have reached the bracket of 'developed countries'. Already, a huge perception of the population in Africa has managed to escape extreme poverty. Even for those who will be the last to escape extreme poverty, they will remain in extreme poverty for much longer, not because it is their destiny, but because of conflict and harsh environmental conditions.

The same goes for religion. It was assumed that the number of babies per woman was dependent on religion, and that women in certain religions would keep having more babies per woman. However, careful analysis of the data shows that the number of babies per woman depends not on religion, but on income levels. Rosling uses several other examples to show that things do not always remain as they have been. The examples include the rise of strong support for women rights in Sweden, as well as increased liberalism around sex and contraception.

To control the destiny instinct, Rosling urges readers to recognize that slow change does not mean that no change is happening. He also urges readers to always be ready to update their knowledge, since knowledge is never constant when it comes to the social sciences. In addition, he urges readers to collect examples of cultural change. He closes by noting that factfulness is recognizing that many things appear to be static just because the change is happening gradually.

KEY TAKEAWAYS:

- The destiny instinct is the tendency to assume that the destinies of people, cultures, countries or religions are determined by an innate characteristic of the group.
- The destiny instinct developed as a result of evolution.
- To control the destiny instinct, Rosling urges readers to recognize that slow change does not mean that no change is happening.
- He also urges readers to always be ready to update their knowledge, since knowledge is never constant when it comes to the social sciences. In addition, he urges readers to collect examples of cultural change.
- Factfulness is recognizing that many things appear to be static just because the change is happening gradually.

Chapter Eight: The Single Perspective Instinct

Rosling starts this chapter by warning the reader against relying on the media to form their worldview. He compares it to forming a view about a person by looking at a picture of their foot. The foot is not one of the best looking parts of the body. Similarly, what is reported in the media is hardly the best things happening in the world. Rosling then introduces the single perspective instinct, the tendency by humans to rely on a simple idea to explain things. It is the preference for single causes and single solutions. However, the world is a lot more complicated. By relying on the single cause and single solution view, we end up misunderstanding the world completely.

Rosling states that people base their understanding of the world on a single perspective for two reasons – professional and political ideology. People who are experts in a certain field will always view all problems from their perspective, just like a child with a hammer will see everything as a nail. Sometimes, even experts have a wrong perspective of their field. For instance, after polling a group of activists for women's rights, Rosling found out that only 8% knew that 30-year-old women have spent just one year less in school on average than 30-year-old men. The activists were so intent on showing that the situation was bad that they did not know of the progress that their activism had brought about. Similarly, many people who support conservation efforts are so focused on the idea that animal species are dying that they do not know of the progress being made. Many other activists – human rights, child protection, women's rights, climate conservation, catastrophe relief, and so on – raise awareness by painting the picture that things are getting worse. However, many are not aware of the progress that is being made. If they ditched the single perspective that things are getting worse and adopted the willingness to show that progress is being made, they could garner even more support for their causes.

Rosling argues that there is never a single way of looking at things. For instance, many people love using numbers to understand situations. However, numbers are not the single solution. Sometimes, numbers do not provide any understanding of the reality behind the numbers. In 2002, Rosling had a chat with Pascaol Mocumbi, the then prime minister of Mozambique. Mocumbi stated that Mozambique was making economic progress. Rosling, however, pointed out that the numbers did not paint such a picture. Mocumbi answered that he did not rely on numbers only to understand his country's economic status. Instead, he also looked at the shoes people wore during the May 1st march. If people are barefoot or have bad shoes, it shows that they have no money. If they have good shoes, it shows that they have money. Similarly, the prime minister looked at construction projects around the country. If the construction projects are going well, it means that people have surplus money to invest. However, if grass is growing over foundations, it means the people have no money.

To explain why there is never a single perspective to any situation, Rosling recounts his experience presenting to the Ministry of Health in Havana, Cuba. After concluding his presentation about how Cuba had a child survival rate almost similar to that of the US at a quarter of the income, the Cuban Minister of Health summarized Rosling's presentation with the statement that, "Cuba is the healthiest of the poor". People applauded this great summary. However, after the presentation, a young man approached Rosling and told him that the Minister of Health had gotten it all wrong. Cuba was not the healthiest of the poor. Instead, he thought Cuba was the poorest of the healthy.

Rosling closes the chapter by stating that factfulness is realizing that a single perspective can limit your imagination. Instead, people should look at situations from multiple angles in order to have a better understanding of the situation.

KEY TAKEAWAYS:

- The single perspective instinct is the tendency by humans to rely on a simple idea to explain things.
- The world is a lot more complicated. By relying on the single cause and single solution view, we end up misunderstanding the world completely.
- People base their understanding of the world on a single perspective for two reasons – professional and political ideology.
- Rosling argues that there is never a single way of looking at things.
- Factfulness is realizing that a single perspective can limit your imagination. Instead, people should look at situations from multiple angles in order to have a better understanding of the situation.

Chapter Nine: The Blame Instinct

The blame instinct is the tendency to look for a simple and clear explanation as to why something bad happened. Whenever things go wrong, it is human nature to assume that it happened as a result of the actions of an individual with malicious intentions. The blame instinct makes us attach a lot of significance or importance to certain individuals or groups. It also denies us the ability to develop a factual understanding of the world. Once we find someone to lay the blame on, we stop looking for the actual cause of the problem and instead focus on punishing the one we think was the cause of the problem. The result is that we undermine our capability to solve the problem and prevent it from occurring again.

For instance, it might be easy to blame a sleepy pilot after a plane crash. However, this does not prevent another pilot from falling asleep inside the cockpit. Instead, it would be much better to spend time to understand why the pilot was asleep and what can be done to ensure another pilot does not sleep while flying a plane. The blame instinct is also accompanied by the 'claim' instinct, the tendency to claim an achievement or credit a specific person or group when something goes well, even if the activity behind the result was a lot more complicated.

Rosling argues that the blame instinct is a reflection of our preferences. We love pointing fingers if we feel it will confirm our existing beliefs. For instance, when UNICEF hired Rosling to investigate a bid for a contract to provide malaria tablets in Angola, his suspicions were awakened. He assumed that the company was trying to fleece UNICEF. Even before he started the investigations, Rosling had started pointing fingers at the company that submitted the bid. The blame instinct created in his mind the idea that UNICEF were the good guys while the company were dishonest. Luckily, it turned out that the company that submitted the bid were running an honest business with a very innovative business model.

To explain the blame instinct, Rosling talks about the cases of refugees who drown in the Mediterranean Sea while trying to reach Europe in inflatable dinghies. Whenever a case of such drowning is reported in the media, fingers are quickly pointed to the smugglers who charge refugees thousands of Euros for a ticket on an inflatable death trap. However, deeper investigation would reveal that the problem is not the smugglers, but rather European immigration policies, which claim that airlines that bring in illegal immigrants must cater for the cost of returning the person to their country of origin.

Since airlines cannot ascertain whether someone is a refugee or not, in a matter of minutes, they deny entry to anyone without a visa. Therefore, refugees, who have a right to enter Europe under the Geneva Convention, cannot do so by plane, despite this being the cheaper and safer option. In addition, any boats that bring in refugees by sea get confiscated by European authorities, so smugglers turn to using cheap inflatable dinghies to transport the refugees, since they cannot afford losing expensive boats after a single trip. The result is that thousands of people die while crossing the Mediterranean Sea in the inflatable dinghies. European countries, which claim to be honoring the Geneva Convention, lay the blame on the smugglers while the actual cause of the problem is their immigration policies. The policies enable the thriving existence of the transport market for the smugglers.

Rosling gives several other examples of the blame instinct and its partner, the claim instinct. For instance, the low birth rate in Asia is credited to Mao's one child policy, when the birth rates actually started falling before the policy was enforced. Instead of giving credit for progress to powerful leaders, Rosling suggests that the credit should be given to institutions and technology, which are the two systems that bring progress to any society. Even societies with incapable leaders will make some progress provided institutions and technology are in place. Rosling ends the chapter by stating that factfulness is recognizing when a scapegoat is being used and realizing that it stops people from finding the actual cause of the problem and coming up with solutions that can prevent similar problems in the future.

KEY TAKEAWAYS:

- The blame instinct is the tendency to look for a simple and clear explanation as to why something bad happened.
- The blame instinct denies us the ability to develop a factual understanding of the world. Once we find someone to lay the blame on, we stop looking for the actual cause of the problem and instead focus on punishing the one we think was the cause of the problem. The result is that we undermine our capability to solve the problem and prevent it from occurring again.
- The blame instinct is a reflection of our preferences. We love pointing fingers if we feel it will confirm our existing beliefs.
- Factfulness is recognizing when a scapegoat is being used and realizing that it stops people from finding the actual cause of the problem and coming up with solutions that can prevent similar problems in the future.

Chapter Ten: The Urgency Instinct

Rosling starts the chapter by recounting his time as a doctor in Nacala district, Mozambique. An unexplained disease had broken out in a poor coastal village which made the legs of patients paralyzed within minutes of onset, and in some cases even made people blind. Rosling wasn't 100% sure whether the disease was contagious. However, the mayor, gripped with a sense of urgency, concluded that something had to be done immediately to prevent the disease from reaching the city. The mayor ordered the military to set up a roadblock to prevent buses from the village travelling to the city. Unable to reach the market within the city by bus, women from the village asked fishermen to take them to the city by sea. Many of the boats, carrying excess passengers, capsized at sea and many women and their children drowned. After further research, Rosling found out that the disease was caused by eating unprocessed cassava. Asking the military to block the buses had caused the death of several women and children, even though the disease was not contagious. The decision to block the road had been driven by the urgency instinct.

The urgency instinct, which is the final instinct, results from thinking that something has to be done now or never. When people are afraid and under compulsion to act immediately, their minds conjure worst case scenarios, leading to very stupid decisions. The urge to make a quick decision supersedes the ability to think analytically. Urgency is something that salesmen and activists have perfected. When salesmen give limited time offers, they are trying to trigger the urgency instinct.

The urgency instinct developed through millions of years of evolution. The instinct spurs us to take immediate action in the face of imminent danger. When our ancestors were living in the bush, it did not make much sense to start analyzing logically when they thought there was a lion in the grass. The safe option was to take off immediately. Even today, the instinct still helps us, for instance when the driver in front of you stops abruptly and you have to swerve immediately or ram into them. However, this instinct can also mess with our understanding of the world.

Many activists try to spur people into action by triggering the urgency instinct. They provide people with worst case scenarios so that people can see the urgency of the matter and the need for immediate action. However, Rosling argues that this should not be the way to go. Using fear and exaggerated data might make people numb to the risks that activists are creating awareness about, leading to inaction instead of action. Instead, he argues that action should be based on data. For instance, many countries claim to be committed in the fight against climate change. However, Rosling found that most countries do not measure their CO_2 emissions regularly. How can countries be committed to fighting a problem if they are not even tracking their progress?

According to Rosling, there are five global risks that the world should worry about; global pandemic, financial collapse, world war, climate change and extreme poverty. Three of these risks have actually happened before, while the last two are happening now. However, he feels that, for solutions to be found, these risks should be approached through cool headed, data based and factual analysis, rather than through drastic action. Trying to create fear through exaggerated alarm is like crying wolf. It can lead to these serious risks being ignored, despite their huge potential of bringing about mass human suffering. Rosling is not saying that we should not worry. However, he is urging the reader to worry about the right thing. He closes the chapter by stating that factfulness is recognizing situations that seem to require urgent, drastic action and realizing that things might not be as urgent as they seem.

KEY TAKEAWAYS:

- The urgency instinct results from thinking that something has to be done now or never.
- When people are afraid and under compulsion to act immediately, their minds conjure worst case scenarios, leading to very stupid decisions. The urge to make a quick decision supersedes the ability to think analytically.
- Urgency is something that salesmen and activists have perfected. When salesmen give limited time offers, they are trying to trigger the urgency instinct.
- Using fear and exaggerated data might make people numb to the risks that activists are creating awareness about, leading to inaction instead of action.
- Instead, action should be based on data.
- According to Rosling, there are five global risks that the world should worry about; global pandemic, financial collapse, world war, climate change and extreme poverty.
- These risks should be approached through cool headed, data based and factual analysis, rather than through drastic action.
- Factfulness is recognizing situations that seem to require urgent, drastic action and realizing that things might not be as urgent as they seem.

Chapter Eleven: Factfulness In Practice

Rosling starts this chapter by recounting a situation that happened in the remote village of Makanga in the DRC. Rosling had travelled to the village to research konzo, the disease caused by unprocessed cassava. The villagers thought that Rosling had come to collect their blood with the intention of selling it, and they were not getting anything out of it. They were baying for his blood, brandishing machetes and shouting at him. Most of the instincts discussed in this book had been triggered. The sharp needles, blood and disease had triggered the fear instinct. The generalization instinct had made them categorize Rosling as a plundering white man. The blame instinct made them assume that he was up to no good. The urgency instinct made the crowd assume that they had to act immediately to prevent this white doctor from exploiting them. It took an old woman from the village to calm the crowd down and explain to them that the doctor was trying to help them, to prevent their children from getting crippled by konzo. Despite her apparent illiteracy, the woman brought factfulness to the whole encounter, thereby saving the lives of Rosling and his translator.

Just like the woman put factfulness into practice in a remote village in the Democratic Republic of Congo, factfulness can also be put into practice in our daily lives – in education, in business, in journalism, in organizations and communities, and even in our individual lives. Children in schools should be taught to adopt an up-to-date, fact-based approach to life. This would help them develop a better perception of the world, which would in turn help them come up with better solutions for the world's problems. Children should be taught how to be curious. They should be taught how to hold two ideas at the same time, and how to be ready to change their opinions when they discover new facts. Doing so will protect the next generation from a lot of ignorance.

Factfulness is also useful in business. Today, having a typo in your CV can keep you from getting a job, yet people who are employed to make policies are placing a billion people on the wrong continent. Businesses are operating using outdated and distorted world views. Businesses in Europe and the United States need to understand that the world markets of the future are currently growing in Africa and Asia. Today, being an American or European company is not a privilege that companies can use to attract international employees. Investors need to shake off their misconceptions about Africa and realize that some African countries present some of the best investment opportunities today.

By adopting factfulness, journalists will become become aware of their dramatic worldviews, thereby helping them present a more accurate worldview to us. However, we cannot expect journalists to start reporting the mundane over the unusual. Instead, it is up to news consumers to start consuming news more factually.

If people are so ignorant of facts at the global level, there is a high likelihood that they are also ignorant of facts at local levels, within the country, and within companies and organizations. This means that there is a high likelihood that countries, organizations and companies are using wrong data to plan for resources, prepare for disasters, find business, and so on. Rosling ends the chapter by asking leaders in countries, cities, companies and organizations to carry out fact based surveys and discover ignorance that exists in their countries, cities, companies and organizations. Only by doing so will people be able to upgrade their worldviews.

KEY TAKEAWAYS

Factfulness can be put into practice in our daily lives – in education, in business, in journalism, in organizations and communities, and even in our individual lives.

Conclusion

This book has forever altered the way I view a great deal of things in life. To ensure the lessons stick, I like to go over just the key takeaways at the end of each chapter once a week. I do this for this book and all the other summaries I've wrote to ensure the key principles are really engrained into my mind and soon become natural habits and reactions in my every day life.

Thanks for checking out my book. I hope you found this of value and enjoyed it. But before you go, I have one small favor to ask…

Would you take 60 seconds and write a review about this book on Amazon?

Reviews are the best way for independent authors (like me) to get noticed, sell more books, and it gives me the motivation to continue producing. I also read every review and use the feedback to write future revisions – and even future books. Thanks again.

Made in the USA
San Bernardino, CA
18 November 2018